The Online Business Buying Blueprint

How to Find, Analyze, and Negotiate Profitable Online Businesses—Even If You're a Complete Beginner

By Joe Correa

Published by Live Stronger Faster

This book is for educational and informational purposes only. The author and publisher are not engaged in rendering legal, financial, or other professional advice. Readers should consult a qualified professional before making any financial decisions.

First Edition

Table of Contents

Introduction

Welcome to the Blueprint That Can Change Your Life

Most people believe that starting a business from scratch is the only way to become an entrepreneur. The truth? It's not. In fact, it's not even the smartest path for most people. The real shortcut—one that the world's wealthiest investors use—is buying an existing, profitable business that's already working.

This book is designed to show you how to do just that—even if you're a complete beginner.

I created *The Online Business Buying Blueprint* for people like you: aspiring entrepreneurs, side hustlers, freedom seekers, and investors who don't have time to build something from the ground up, but who want income, independence, and impact. If you've ever dreamed of owning an online business—whether it's an eCommerce store, a course-based empire, a SaaS company, or a content site—this book is your step-by-step roadmap.

Why Buy Instead of Build?

Building a business from scratch is risky. You're unproven. You don't have traffic. You don't know if your product will work. But when you buy a business, you're starting on third base. The traffic, the customers, the revenue—they're already there. You're not guessing. You're growing.

In this book, you'll learn how to:

- Identify the best online businesses to buy based on your goals and lifestyle
- Analyze financials, traffic sources, customer bases, and red flags
- Avoid scams and overpriced listings
- Negotiate like a pro (even if you've never bought anything more expensive than a used car)
- Structure a deal with limited cash upfront (yes, it's possible!)
- Run and grow the business once it's yours

And the best part? You don't need a Harvard MBA, a massive budget, or a tech background to do this. All you need is the willingness to learn, analyze, and take action.

My Journey: From Curious Observer to Business Owner

Years ago, I stumbled upon a website marketplace. At first, I was just curious. I didn't even know people sold websites. But after diving in, I realized something profound: digital real estate was exploding. And the entry points were way more accessible than I imagined. Some businesses were selling for as little as $2,000. Others for millions.

I decided to go all in. I bought my first content website for under $5,000. It wasn't flashy. But it was making a couple hundred dollars a month in passive income. Over time, I learned how to analyze better deals, negotiate better prices, and eventually buy bigger, more profitable online businesses.

Fast-forward to today: I've been part of deals ranging from small affiliate sites to 6-figure educational platforms. And now I want to share what I've learned with you—so you can skip the painful trial and error.

Who This Book Is For

- You're a 9-to-5 employee who wants to escape the grind
- You're a stay-at-home parent looking for flexible income
- You're a digital nomad searching for portable cash flow
- You're an investor who wants cash-producing digital assets

- Or you're just someone who knows there's more to life than a paycheck

No matter your background, if you're willing to follow this blueprint, you'll be able to make your first acquisition within the next 30–90 days.

Let's Talk About the Elephant in the Room: Fear

Yes, buying a business sounds scary. There's money involved. What if it fails? What if you get ripped off? These fears are normal. And valid. But that's why this book exists. I'll walk you through the due diligence process. I'll show you how to ask the right questions, interpret financials, and spot BS from a mile away.

By the end of this book, you'll feel confident navigating marketplaces like Flippa, Empire Flippers, and MicroAcquire. You'll know what to look for, what to avoid, and how to turn a single business into a life-changing asset.

What's Inside

Here's a sneak peek of what you'll learn:

- **Chapter 1:** Why Buying Beats Building

- **Chapter 2:** The 5 Types of Online Businesses You Can Buy
- **Chapter 3:** Where to Find Great Deals (and How to Vet Them)
- **Chapter 4:** The Financials: Profit, Trends, Traffic, and Risks
- **Chapter 5:** Deal Structuring: How to Pay Less (and Smarter)
- **Chapter 6:** Due Diligence Checklist
- **Chapter 7:** Negotiation Secrets That Actually Work
- **Chapter 8:** What to Do the First 30 Days After You Buy
- **Chapter 9:** Scaling and Exit Planning
- **Chapter 10:** Creative Ways to Fund Your First Acquisition

Let's Get Started

You're not just buying a business—you're buying back your time, your freedom, and your future. Let's take that first step together. Turn the page, hit play, and let's dive in.

Chapter 1: Why Buying Beats Building

"You don't need to start from zero. You need to start from smart."

The Harsh Reality of Starting from Scratch

Before we dive into how to buy a business, let's break down the reasons why most new online businesses fail—and why buying a business avoids 80% of those pitfalls.

- Common Problems with Building From Scratch:

1. **No Proof of Concept** You don't know if your idea will actually work. You may build a product no one wants.

2. **Zero Traffic** New sites don't rank in search engines, and social media takes months (or years) to build. Expect crickets.

3. **Cash Burn Without Revenue** You'll spend money—on domains, hosting, content, tools—but may see no ROI for 6–12 months or longer.

4. **Marketing Guesswork** You're starting with no email list, no customer feedback, no reviews, no ads—just you and trial and error.

5. **Loneliness and Burnout** Building a startup alone is

exhausting. The lack of early momentum often leads to giving up too soon.

- ❖ **KEY INSIGHT:** The road to success is not just hard—it's long and uncertain. Buying skips many of the hardest steps.

The 7 Major Advantages of Buying an Online Business

Now let's look at what you actually get when you buy instead of build.

Advantage 1: Immediate Cash Flow

You skip the startup phase and begin with revenue from day one. You're buying *proof* of concept.

Advantage 2: Proven Product & Market Fit

If the business is making sales, it already has a product or service that customers want. You don't have to guess.

Advantage 3: Built-In Traffic

Whether it's SEO, email subscribers, or paid ads, the traffic systems are already in place.

Advantage 4: Existing Customers & Data

You get access to a database of past buyers, abandoned carts, user behavior, and repeat customers.

Advantage 5: Brand Reputation

Even if small, the business has a name, some recognition, and likely social proof like testimonials and reviews.

Advantage 6: Smoother Scaling

Because the systems already work, your focus is on optimization and growth—not building everything from the ground up.

Advantage 7: Faster ROI

With existing income and traffic, your ability to recoup your investment is significantly faster than starting from zero.

- ❖ **ACTION STEP:** Write down your income goal (e.g., $2,000/month). Then research 3 businesses that already generate that on platforms like Flippa or Acquire.com.

The Myth of "It's Cheaper to Start"

People assume building is cheaper because you're not "buying" anything. But consider the *real* costs:

Startup Costs Most People Overlook:

- Website setup ($500–$1,000)
- Copywriting & branding ($500–$2,000)
- SEO tools & content creation ($200/month)
- Time spent learning and testing (hundreds of hours)

After 6–12 months, you might still have no revenue. In contrast, a $10,000 purchase of a business making $500/month could pay for itself in under two years.

❖ **ACTION STEP:** List all the time, money, and effort you've spent trying to start something. Ask yourself: Would it have been smarter to buy a business already working?

The Risk Argument — Which Is Really Riskier?

Here's a common objection:

> "Buying is risky! What if the business fails after I buy it?"

That's a fair concern. But let's compare the risks.

Starting From Scratch	**Buying a Business**
90% failure rate	25–30% failure (after due diligence)
No data to evaluate	Full traffic, profit, & conversion history
No income for months	Immediate revenue potential
Unpredictable costs	Clear financial records
Untested product or market	Proven customer demand

When done properly with solid due diligence (we'll show you how in Chapter 6), **buying is the *lower-risk* option.**

INSIGHT: Smart investors don't gamble—they mitigate risk. Your job is to become a skilled buyer, not a blind one.

Real-World Example – From $0 to $1,200/Month in 30 Days

Let's take an example. Jason was a digital marketing consultant with no product to sell. He wanted a side income stream but didn't want to spend 6 months learning SEO and building a blog.

He bought a content site making $600/month through display ads and affiliate links. He negotiated the price down to $9,000.

Within 30 days, he had:

- Cleaned up broken links
- Added new high-converting articles
- Doubled the affiliate earnings

The site now makes over $1,200/month passively.

ROI: 13 months to break even. After that, pure profit. **Time invested:** About 10 hours total.

What Makes a Good First Acquisition

You don't need to buy a $100K SaaS platform. You can start small.

For Beginners, Look for:

- **Low-maintenance content sites** with SEO traffic
- **Simple eCommerce stores** using dropshipping
- **Micro-SaaS products** with low support needs

- **Online courses** or digital product libraries
- **Email list or PLR-based businesses**

Start with businesses between $2,000–$20,000. Lower price = lower risk. Focus on learning the process.

- ❖ **ACTION STEP:** Browse 3–5 listings today and identify what's being sold, how much it earns, and why the owner is selling.

Final Takeaway from Chapter 1

Buying an online business isn't just a "shortcut." It's a strategic, scalable, and safer path to financial freedom. It removes 80% of the guesswork and 90% of the failure rate. But like any investment, it requires knowledge.

The good news? You're already ahead of 99% of people just by reading this book.

Chapter 1 Recap

- Building from scratch is time-consuming, risky, and full of unknowns.
- Buying skips the hardest parts: no product testing, no traffic building, and no waiting for revenue.

- It's not risk-free, but it's far more predictable and scalable with proper due diligence.
- Start with a small acquisition to learn the process before going bigger.

Chapter 2: The 5 Types of Online Businesses You Can Buy

> *"Your first acquisition doesn't need to be perfect. It just needs to match your skills, time, and income goals."*

Not all online businesses are created equal. Some require daily attention, others run almost passively. Some are content-heavy, while others rely on software or physical products. Choosing the *right* business model is step one in becoming a successful online business buyer.

In this chapter, you'll learn the 5 most common and beginner-friendly types of online businesses, how each works, the pros and cons, and which one is best for *your* goals and skill set.

1. Content Sites (Blogs, Niche Websites, Affiliate Sites)

These are websites that make money through articles, SEO traffic, and monetization like display ads and affiliate links.

How They Make Money:

- Google AdSense or platforms like Ezoic/MediaVine
- Amazon Associates or affiliate programs

- Sponsored posts or product placements
- Selling digital downloads or info products

Pros:

- Passive income once set up
- Easy to understand and manage
- Low overhead (hosting, content updates)
- Great for beginners with writing or SEO skills

Cons:

- SEO traffic can fluctuate
- Income may be slow to grow
- Needs content upkeep and link-building

Best For:

- Writers, bloggers, digital marketers, hobbyists
- People with limited time and low upfront capital

❖ **Example Listing**: "PetCareTips.com – $500/month passive income from ads & affiliate links, asking price $10,000"

2. E-Commerce Stores (Physical or Dropshipping Products)

E-commerce stores sell physical products through Shopify, WooCommerce, or marketplaces like Amazon.

How They Make Money:

- Direct product sales
- Bundles or upsells
- Subscription products
- Print-on-demand or dropshipping

Pros:

- High revenue potential
- Easier to scale with paid ads
- Dropshipping can reduce inventory risks

Cons:

- More moving parts: shipping, inventory, returns
- Customer service demands
- Advertising costs can cut into profit margins

Best For:

- Hands-on operators, marketers, product designers
- Those with experience in logistics or retail

❖ **Example Listing**: "SmartYogaGear.com – $2,500/month profit, 80% dropshipping, asking price $38,000"

3. SaaS Businesses (Software as a Service)

These businesses offer a software tool or app for a monthly or annual subscription fee.

How They Make Money:

- Recurring subscriptions
- Tiered pricing plans
- Freemium-to-paid upgrades

Pros:

- High profit margins (after development)
- Predictable, recurring income
- Very scalable

Cons:

- Requires tech knowledge or a developer
- Ongoing bug fixes, updates, and customer support
- Can be complex to evaluate without experience

Best For:

- Developers, tech-savvy operators, or those with access to a tech team
- Investors looking for monthly recurring revenue (MRR)

❖ **Example Listing**: "InvoicelyPro – $1,200/month in MRR, 150 active users, asking price $22,000"

4. Digital Product Businesses (Courses, Templates, Memberships)

These businesses sell digital assets like online courses, eBooks, or paid memberships—often hosted on platforms like Kajabi, Teachable, or Gumroad.

How They Make Money:

- One-time or recurring sales
- Tiered access or bundle offers

- Upsells and add-on products

Pros:

- No physical fulfillment or inventory
- High margins (digital = near-zero cost)
- Easy to scale with ads or partnerships

Cons:

- May rely heavily on the personal brand of the seller
- Requires marketing and funnel optimization
- Course content may need updating over time

Best For:

- Teachers, coaches, creators, influencers
- Buyers with marketing experience or email list access

❖ **Example Listing**: "RemoteWriterAcademy.com – $4,000/month revenue from writing courses, asking price $60,000"

5. Marketplace or Directory Sites

These are platforms that connect two parties (like buyers and sellers or service providers and clients), often monetized through listing fees, memberships, or commissions.

How They Make Money:

- Paid listings
- Featured upgrades
- Advertising or affiliate links
- Membership or subscription access

Pros:

- Unique niche opportunities
- Can generate recurring revenue
- Less content maintenance than blogs

Cons:

- May need strong SEO or PPC to keep traffic steady
- Not as passive as content sites
- Niche marketplaces may have limited buyer interest

Best For:

- People with niche expertise or access to industry contacts
- Buyers who want recurring income and are okay with admin tasks

❖ **Example Listing**: "TutorMatchOnline.com – $800/month in memberships, asking price $12,000"

How to Choose the Right Type for YOU

The best type of business to buy depends on 3 key factors:

1. Your Available Time

- 1–5 hrs/week: Go for content sites or digital product businesses
- 10+ hrs/week: Consider eCommerce or marketplace businesses

2. Your Skills

- SEO or writing? ➜ Content sites
- Marketing or email funnels? ➜ Digital products
- Tech/dev experience? ➜ SaaS

- Customer service or retail? ➔ E-commerce

3. Your Risk Tolerance & Budget

- $2,000–$10,000: Start with content or affiliate sites
- $10,000–$50,000: Digital products, eCommerce, small SaaS
- $50,000+: Subscription SaaS, larger content or course businesses

❖ **ACTION STEP:** Rank the 5 models from most to least appealing for your lifestyle. Then search for 2 real listings that fit your top choice.

What to Avoid as a Beginner

Avoid business types that:

- Rely heavily on the founder's personal brand
- Require custom software with no documentation
- Are declining in traffic or revenue
- Have vague or unverifiable numbers
- Are priced too high for their profit level (bad ROI)

You'll learn how to vet these more thoroughly in the due diligence chapter—but awareness starts now.

Chapter 2 Recap:

- There are 5 main types of online businesses: Content Sites, E-commerce, SaaS, Digital Products, and Marketplaces
- Each has unique pros, cons, and workload
- Your skills, time, and capital should dictate which is best for you
- You can start with as little as $2,000 and scale over time
- Focus on simplicity, profitability, and sustainability

In the next chapter, we'll dive into **where** to actually find these deals, **how to read the listings**, and **what red flags to look for** before making your move.

Chapter 3: Where to Find Great Deals (and How to Vet Them)

"If you know where to look—and what to look for—you'll always find opportunity."

Once you understand the types of online businesses available, the next step is knowing *where* to find them and *how* to separate the good from the bad. Think of this chapter as your treasure map. We're going to cover the best platforms to source online businesses, how to quickly analyze a listing, and the biggest red flags that should stop you in your tracks. This is where theory meets action—because browsing listings is how you'll build your buying instincts.

There are two main ways to find online businesses for sale: marketplaces and brokerages. Marketplaces are like eBay for digital businesses. They list hundreds of businesses of all types, from content sites making $100 a month to full-blown SaaS platforms earning six figures annually. The listings are public, and buyers can message sellers directly. Popular marketplaces include **Flippa**, **Acquire.com**, **SideProjectors**, and **IndieMaker**. These are great for beginners because they have lower entry points, tons of listings, and helpful filters for finding deals in your price range.

On the other hand, brokerages operate more like real estate agents. They vet the sellers, verify financials, and provide a higher level of service—usually for more mature or expensive businesses. Top brokerages include **Empire Flippers**, **FE International**, **Quiet Light**, and **Motion Invest**. These platforms often specialize in content sites, Amazon FBA businesses, eCommerce stores, and SaaS companies. The listings usually include detailed prospectuses, interviews with sellers, and some level of due diligence already done. The tradeoff? You'll typically pay more. But the risk is often lower because the businesses are better vetted.

Regardless of where you search, it's important to approach each listing with a healthy dose of curiosity and skepticism. You are not just shopping—you're *investigating*. The first thing to check in a listing is the profit. Not revenue—**profit**. Revenue might sound impressive, but it's the net monthly income that matters. For example, a business that makes $10,000 per month in revenue but has $9,500 in expenses is only earning $500 in profit. That's the number you want to focus on.

Next, look for consistency. Is the profit stable month to month, or are there huge spikes and drops? A consistent track record is a green flag. Look at traffic sources: are visitors coming from SEO, email, paid ads, or social media? A business that depends

100% on paid ads is riskier because traffic can vanish if ad costs rise or performance drops. On the other hand, organic traffic or a strong email list is more stable and scalable.

Another important factor is the age of the business. A site that's been around for 2+ years and is still profitable is more trustworthy than one that popped up six months ago. Time is a validator. It proves sustainability. You'll also want to understand the seller's reason for selling. Sometimes it's a good reason—like moving to another project or wanting to cash out. But be cautious if the reason is vague or evasive. "Burned out" or "personal reasons" might be legit, but dig deeper. Ask follow-up questions. What's the workload like? What's the current owner's daily or weekly involvement? A business that requires 20 hours a week may be fine for some—but not if you're looking for something passive.

Many listings will use a multiple of monthly profit to calculate the asking price. A business making $1,000/month may sell for 30x its monthly profit, or $30,000. This is a common valuation method in the online business world. The multiple usually ranges from 20x to 45x depending on the niche, age, stability, traffic, and complexity of the business. Lower multiples may indicate higher risk—or a motivated seller. Higher multiples usually reflect quality and predictability.

To evaluate listings efficiently, create a simple spreadsheet. Include columns like "Business Name," "Platform," "Monthly Profit," "Asking Price," "Profit Multiple," "Traffic Source," "Owner Time Commitment," and "My Interest Level." This turns browsing into a data-driven habit. You'll start to notice patterns: which niches perform better, what prices are typical, and how listings are structured. This awareness is critical before you ever make your first offer.

Now let's talk about red flags—the warning signs that should either pause your interest or stop it altogether. The biggest red flag is unverifiable income. If the seller won't provide screenshots, access to analytics, or proof of revenue, walk away. Transparency is a must. Another major red flag is unexplained traffic drops. If a site's traffic plummeted recently due to a Google update or ad ban, be cautious. You don't want to inherit someone else's unsolvable problem.

Also, avoid businesses with poor documentation. If there are no SOPs (standard operating procedures), unclear customer acquisition funnels, or missing financial records, it will take you months just to figure out how the business runs. And that's assuming it's even salvageable. One of the most overlooked red flags is seller dependency. If the business's success relies heavily on the seller's personality, expertise, or relationships (like a personal brand or YouTube channel with their face), it may be difficult to replicate results once you take over.

If you're serious about buying, you'll eventually want to reach out to sellers. This is your chance to ask the right questions. Here are a few good ones to start with:

- Why are you selling the business now?
- How much time do you currently spend on the business each week?
- What would you do if you kept the business?
- What are the biggest growth opportunities?
- What skills are required to maintain or grow it?
- Are there any risks or challenges a new owner should know about?

These questions serve two purposes. First, they help you understand the business more deeply. Second, they help you gauge the *seller's transparency.* A good seller will welcome your questions and provide thoughtful answers. A sketchy one will dodge, deflect, or disappear.

It's also worth noting that some of the best deals never go public. This is known as the "off-market" world of online business buying. These are deals you can find by networking in niche Facebook groups, joining private Slack or Discord communities for founders, or cold-emailing operators of small websites or stores. If you see a website you like, consider reaching out and asking if they'd be open to selling. You'd be surprised how many will entertain the idea, especially if they've plateaued or lost interest in growing it further.

Finally, patience pays. Don't rush to buy the first shiny object you see. Browse regularly. Track trends. Ask questions. Wait for the right fit. And most importantly, remember: you're not just buying a website. You're buying time, income, opportunity, and freedom. Treat each potential purchase like a long-term partnership. Because when you find the right business, it's not just a transaction—it's a transformation.

In the next chapter, we'll break down how to analyze financials, traffic metrics, and customer data in detail so you can make smart, confident decisions before you ever write a check or send a wire.

Chapter 4: The Financials – Profit, Trends, Traffic, and Risks

"If the numbers don't work, nothing else matters."

Financials are the heartbeat of any business. You might love the brand name, admire the design, or get excited about its niche—but if the numbers aren't solid, it's a ticking time bomb. In this chapter, we're going to dissect the four pillars you must evaluate before making an offer: **profit**, **trends**, **traffic**, and **risk factors**. Together, these elements tell the true story of the business you're considering buying.

Let's begin with the most obvious metric: **profit**. This is not the same as revenue. Revenue is how much money the business *brings in*. Profit is what's *left over* after all expenses are paid. The two can look drastically different. A dropshipping store might show $30,000 per month in revenue, but after deducting product costs, ads, apps, and refunds, it could be netting just $1,000. On the flip side, a small blog generating $2,000 a month from ad revenue and costing only $100 in hosting could be pulling in $1,900 in profit. Always start with net profit, not top-line sales.

To calculate a business's profitability, you'll need access to the seller's profit and loss (P&L) statements, or at the very least, a detailed spreadsheet of monthly income and expenses. Ideally, you want to review 12–24 months of financial history. This helps you identify trends and seasonality. Is the income growing, flat, or declining? If it's declining, why? Has the seller stopped maintaining it, or is the niche itself losing relevance? Numbers don't lie—but they don't explain themselves either. That's your job.

Now let's talk about **trends**, which are often just as important as the actual profit figure. Imagine you see two content websites, each earning $1,000 a month. One has been flat for 12 months. The other grew from $200 to $1,000 in the last three months. At first glance, the growing site seems better. But ask yourself: is that growth sustainable, or was it a fluke? Was it caused by a temporary viral spike, a seasonal bump, or a short-term ad strategy? Similarly, if a site used to make $1,500/month and is now down to $1,000, you must ask: is it recoverable or in decline?

A great tool for visualizing these patterns is Google Analytics or, in the case of eCommerce, platforms like Shopify or Stripe. Look for traffic consistency. Are there unnatural spikes followed by steep drops? A sudden surge in revenue might be linked to a one-off campaign or promotion. A healthy business shows steady upward or stable trends—not rollercoaster behavior. You want a business with *momentum*, not one that's running out of steam.

Next comes **traffic**, which is arguably the lifeblood of any online business. Where are the visitors coming from? How reliable are those sources? The main traffic channels include organic search (SEO), paid ads, social media, direct traffic, and referrals. Organic traffic is typically the most valuable—it's free, consistent, and less likely to disappear overnight. Paid ads, on the other hand, can drive fast growth but also carry higher risk. If a business depends entirely on Facebook or Google Ads, its profits are vulnerable to rising ad costs or declining performance.

Check the traffic mix. Ideally, you want diversified sources. If 90% of traffic comes from one blog post or one keyword, that's a red flag. If a YouTube channel drives all the traffic but the seller is the face of the brand, you'll need to consider whether you can sustain that level of engagement. Ask for full access to Google Analytics, YouTube Studio, or ad dashboards. Look at key metrics like bounce rate, average session duration, and pages per visit. These numbers will tell you whether the audience is truly engaged or just passing through.

Also look at conversion rates—how many visitors are turning into customers or subscribers? For content sites, this might mean email opt-ins or ad impressions per page. For eCommerce, it's the percentage of visitors who complete a purchase. A store with 10,000 visitors a month and a 1% conversion rate is making 100 sales. Improve that to 2% and you've doubled the revenue without touching the traffic. This is why understanding the full customer funnel is crucial before buying.

The final piece of the financial puzzle is **risk**. Every business has it, but your job is to identify and mitigate those risks before purchase. The first major risk is platform dependency. Is the business overly reliant on Amazon, Etsy, Facebook, or Google? If it's an Amazon FBA business and Amazon changes the rules or suspends the account, your income could evaporate. Diversification—across channels, products, and traffic—is one of the strongest signals of long-term stability.

Another risk is operational complexity. Some businesses have strong numbers but require 20–30 hours a week to maintain. If you're looking for a passive or semi-passive investment, that's a mismatch. Ask detailed questions about the owner's role. What exactly do they do every day, week, and month? What tasks could be delegated? Are there SOPs (standard operating procedures) in place? Is there a team that would stay on after the sale? Risk is often hidden in the operations, not just the numbers.

Then there's the issue of customer retention and lifetime value. Does the business rely on new customer acquisition each month, or does it generate repeat sales from existing buyers? A subscription or SaaS model with low churn is much more stable than a one-time-purchase business with high customer turnover. Also ask about refunds, chargebacks, and complaints. High refund rates or poor customer reviews may signal a deeper problem with the product or service.

One often-overlooked financial risk is deferred maintenance. For example, a content site that hasn't added new articles in 12 months might still be earning, but it's living on borrowed time. Google could de-rank outdated content, and competitors may catch up. Similarly, a SaaS product with no recent updates or bug fixes may lose users quickly. Ask the seller: what happens if you do nothing for 30–60 days after buying? If the answer is "It keeps working," great. If the answer is "It crumbles," you have more due diligence to do.

Let's summarize with a short checklist of financial questions to ask before making an offer:

- What is the net monthly profit, and how is it calculated?
- Are financials independently verified (bank, Stripe, PayPal, etc.)?

- How stable is the monthly revenue and profit over the past 12 months?
- What percentage of traffic is organic vs. paid?
- What are the top 3 traffic sources, and how sustainable are they?
- What are the conversion rates and customer acquisition costs?
- What are the biggest expenses, and are they negotiable or avoidable?
- What is the seller's daily or weekly involvement in maintaining the business?
- Are there any customer service complaints or refunds that concern you?
- Is the business currently growing, flat, or declining—and why?

Your goal is to turn data into insight. Don't let big revenue numbers blind you. Focus on margins, sustainability, and ease of transfer. Remember, a business that makes $1,500/month passively and runs on auto-pilot is *far* more valuable to most buyers than one making $5,000/month that requires 40 hours of labor.

When you analyze a business this way—like a professional investor—you stop thinking emotionally and start thinking strategically. That's the mindset that leads to great deals and long-term digital wealth.

In the next chapter, we'll take everything you've learned and show you how to **structure a deal**—even if you don't have all the cash upfront. You'll discover creative ways to fund your first acquisition, negotiate like a pro, and close with confidence.

Chapter 5: Deal Structuring — How to Pay Less (and Smarter)

> *"You don't need a big wallet—you need a smart structure."*

So far, you've learned how to identify the right type of online business, find great deals, and evaluate them based on solid financials. But now comes the big question: **how do you actually afford the purchase?** The good news? You don't always need to pay the full price upfront. In this chapter, you'll learn creative and strategic ways to structure a deal that works for *you*—even if you don't have $50,000 sitting in your bank account.

Most people assume you need to wire the entire asking price in cash to buy an online business. That's only one option. In reality, deal structuring is one of the most powerful tools in your buyer toolkit. Just like in real estate or private equity, online businesses can be purchased with flexible terms: split payments, seller financing, earn-outs, and even revenue-share agreements. Sellers often care more about getting a fair deal and transitioning to the right buyer than receiving every dollar upfront.

Let's start with the simplest model: the **all-cash deal**. In this case, you pay the entire asking price—or a negotiated lower price—in one lump sum. This is the cleanest and fastest way to close a deal. It's also the riskiest for you as a buyer, since you bear 100% of the risk immediately. That said, if the deal is small (say, $2,000 to $10,000), and you've done your due diligence, a full-cash offer can give you leverage to negotiate a discount. Sellers love simplicity, and many will drop their price for a quick close.

But what if the price is higher than your available cash? That's where **seller financing** comes in. This is when the seller agrees to let you pay a portion of the price up front—say 50%—and then pay the rest over time in monthly installments. For example, you might pay $15,000 up front on a $30,000 business, then pay $1,500/month for the next 10 months. This helps preserve your capital while still acquiring the business. And sellers often accept these terms, especially if the business has steady cash flow and they trust your ability to run it.

Another option is the **earn-out** model. With an earn-out, you pay an initial amount up front, and the rest is paid based on the business's future performance. This structure works well when a business has had recent growth or volatility, and the buyer wants to reduce risk. For instance, you might agree to pay $10,000 now, and then an additional $20,000 over 12 months—**only** if the business continues earning at least

$1,500/month. Earn-outs create alignment between buyer and seller: you both benefit from keeping the business healthy during the transition.

If you're short on cash but high on confidence, consider a **revenue share agreement**. In this setup, you agree to pay the seller a percentage of future profits rather than a lump sum. For example, you take over the business and pay 30% of net income for the next 24 months until a target amount is reached. This is a great option for underperforming or neglected assets where the seller no longer wants involvement, and you're willing to do the work. These deals are harder to find but extremely attractive when structured well.

Let's not forget **outside funding options**. If you have decent personal credit or a business entity, you can often use a 0% interest credit card, a personal loan, or a business line of credit to finance the purchase. Some buyers even use home equity lines of credit (HELOCs) or funds from their retirement accounts (via a self-directed IRA or Solo 401(k)) to acquire cash-flowing digital assets. If the business you're buying earns $2,000/month and your loan payment is only $600/month, the cash flow can cover the debt and leave you with profit from day one.

There's also a lesser-known strategy called

acquire-to-partner. In this model, you negotiate with the seller to buy *into* the business as a partial owner—say 50%—and then work your way to 100% ownership over time. This is useful when the seller still wants to stay involved for a limited time or when they're open to you growing the business and paying them out from future profits. You split the workload and risk while benefiting from their knowledge and your new energy.

Whatever structure you use, one thing is key: **negotiation**. Don't assume the listed price is final. Most listings on Flippa, Acquire, or even brokered platforms are negotiable—especially when you're respectful, informed, and clear about your plan. Sellers want to feel good about who's taking over their "baby." That emotional connection can often work in your favor. Be professional, but don't be afraid to ask for better terms. Sometimes, the structure matters more than the total price.

Here are some phrases you can use during negotiation:

- "Would you be open to a split payment: 60% upfront and 40% in 3–6 months?"
- "I'm really interested, but my capital is tied up—would seller financing over 12 months work for you?"

- "Would you consider an earn-out based on revenue milestones to reduce upfront risk for both of us?"
- "I'd love to offer $20,000 all-cash for a fast close. Would that be acceptable if we closed within 7 days?"

Notice how each offer is framed around *mutual benefit*. You're not lowballing—you're creating a win-win. That's the key to successful deal structuring.

Also, don't underestimate the value of non-financial negotiation. Some sellers will accept a lower price if you take over quickly, agree to use their team, or offer a smooth handoff process. Others might accept terms if you include a consulting agreement—paying them to stay on for 30–60 days after the sale to train you or handle the transition. This ensures continuity and gives you time to learn the ropes without pressure.

Always put your agreement in writing. Use a **Letter of Intent (LOI)** to outline the terms before entering due diligence. Then use an **Asset Purchase Agreement (APA)** for the final contract. These documents should clearly spell out the purchase price, structure, payment schedule, transfer of assets, support period, and non-compete clauses. You can find templates online or hire a freelance attorney on Upwork or Fiverr to draft one affordably.

Before you close, make sure you confirm *ownership transfer steps.* This includes domain transfer, website hosting, admin accounts (email, payment processors, content management systems), ad accounts, email list ownership, and access to customer service tools. Missing any of these could cause delays—or worse, loss of access to key revenue drivers.

To sum up: a creative deal structure can open doors you never thought were possible. You don't need to save for five years to buy your first online business. You need to understand how to reduce the upfront burden, protect your downside, and still give the seller a reason to say yes.

In the next chapter, we'll cover **due diligence**—arguably the most important part of the process. You'll learn exactly how to verify claims, validate metrics, and make sure you're not buying a lemon disguised as a gem.

Chapter 6: Due Diligence Checklist

"Due diligence is where deals are made—or regretted."

You've found a business you like, the numbers look solid, and you've even agreed on a deal structure. Great. But before you send any money, you must complete the most important step of all: **due diligence**. This is the part where you dig beneath the surface and verify that everything the seller has claimed is accurate, sustainable, and transferable. It's your opportunity to protect yourself—and your investment—from costly surprises. Think of it as your pre-flight checklist before takeoff. Skipping it is how buyers crash.

At its core, due diligence is about **verification**. You're not taking the seller's word—you're confirming the truth behind every claim. This process should be methodical and thorough, not rushed. It might take a few days or even a couple of weeks, but it's worth every minute. Let's break down the five major categories of due diligence: **financials**, **traffic**, **operations**, **legal/IP**, and **transferability**.

Start with the **financials**. You'll want full access to revenue reports from sources like Stripe, PayPal, Gumroad, Shopify, or any other payment gateway the business uses. Don't settle for screenshots—request read-only access to dashboards, or at minimum, a recorded screen walkthrough from the seller showing real-time revenue and history. Compare these figures to the profit and loss (P&L) statements they've shared. Make sure recurring revenue matches what they claimed and that refund rates aren't excessive.

Next, verify **expenses**. This includes paid software tools, advertising costs, hosting, contractor payments, and any other recurring overhead. Ask for receipts or bank statements if needed. Be sure to separate *necessary* expenses from optional ones. For example, if the seller pays $500/month for premium analytics but you're comfortable with Google Analytics, that's an optional cost. Your goal is to calculate *true net profit*—not inflated figures that depend on unsustainable spending.

After financials, turn to **traffic verification**. If the business relies on website visits, you'll need access to Google Analytics. Make sure traffic is consistent, not spiking from one viral post or paid campaign. Check for red flags like high bounce rates, short session durations, or drops in returning users. For social media–based businesses, examine insights from Facebook, Instagram, YouTube, or TikTok dashboards. Verify that the followers are real and engagement is organic—not the result of paid bots or artificial boosts.

Pay special attention to **traffic sources**. If 80% of visits come from one keyword or one YouTube video, the risk of sudden traffic loss is high. Diversification is your friend. Look for multiple traffic sources contributing to the business's revenue. Ask whether any recent algorithm changes have impacted the site or channel, and how the seller has responded. If paid ads are involved, review the ad account. Are ROAS (return on ad spend) numbers healthy? Are campaigns still active and scalable?

The third area is **operations**. You want to understand exactly how the business runs, day to day. Ask the seller to document their weekly and monthly workflow. What tasks are completed daily? Who handles customer service? How is content produced or orders fulfilled? The goal is to identify what systems are in place—and what still relies on the seller personally. If the business needs 20 hours a week and the seller has been handling everything, you'll need to either invest your own time or hire help.

Ask to see any **Standard Operating Procedures (SOPs)**, templates, and automation tools the seller uses. These are critical for a smooth transition. If they don't exist, that's not a dealbreaker—but it means you'll be spending more time onboarding yourself. Also, evaluate the team. Are there contractors, freelancers, or virtual assistants currently involved? Are they willing to stay after the sale? If yes, clarify their roles, rates, and expectations in writing.

Now comes the **legal and intellectual property (IP)** review. Make sure the business owns everything it claims to. If it's an eCommerce business, confirm trademarks, business registration, supplier contracts, and licenses. For content or digital product businesses, ensure the seller owns the content and has not violated copyright laws. Use plagiarism tools like Copyscape to check original content. Ask about software licenses, affiliate agreements, or partnerships that could be affected by a change in ownership.

It's also critical to check for **pending disputes or legal threats**. Has the business received DMCA takedown notices? Are there unresolved customer complaints, chargebacks, or Better Business Bureau reports? A business that looks clean on the surface could have hidden liabilities that only come out after the sale—when they become *your* problem. Make sure to ask explicitly about any legal issues and have the seller confirm in writing that none exist.

The last and most overlooked category is **transferability**. In other words, will you be able to *run and grow* the business once it's yours? This includes technical transferability—domain names, hosting access, email accounts, payment processors, and platforms like Teachable, Shopify, or WordPress. Get a full list of all assets and make sure the seller agrees to hand over access within 24–48 hours of closing.

Also confirm *relationship* transferability. If the business relies on suppliers, sponsors, or affiliates, will those relationships continue with you? If the seller is well-known in the space and the brand revolves around them personally, that may not transfer cleanly. Ask for warm introductions, transition emails, or calls where appropriate. The more reliant the business is on the seller's personal network or reputation, the more critical this step becomes.

As you go through the due diligence process, document everything. Create a checklist or folder structure where you store financial data, traffic screenshots, contracts, SOPs, and correspondence. This is your due diligence file. If anything feels off, pause. Don't be afraid to ask hard questions or walk away. Remember, a deal that looks too good to be true usually is.

Here's a quick sample due diligence checklist you can use:

Financial:

- 12–24 months of revenue (Stripe, PayPal, Gumroad, etc.)
- P&L statements with monthly breakdowns
- Expense records and receipts
- Bank statements (optional but ideal)

Traffic:

- Google Analytics access (or equivalent)
- Breakdown of traffic sources (SEO, paid, social)
- Bounce rate, time on site, and device types
- Ad account performance data if applicable

Operations:

- SOPs and process documentation
- List of tools, apps, and automation systems
- Weekly and monthly task summaries
- Staff or contractor details

Legal & IP:

- Trademark or copyright ownership (if any)
- Domain registration and hosting access
- Content originality check (Copyscape)
- Affiliate, vendor, or partner agreements

Transferability:

- Full asset list (domains, email, content, software)
- Access to all relevant logins
- Customer list and CRM handoff
- Transition plan and seller support timeline

Finally, don't go it alone if you feel uncertain. You can hire third-party services or consultants who specialize in due diligence for online businesses. Some brokerages offer this as part of the process, while freelancers on platforms like Upwork or MicroAcquire can provide affordable audits for peace of mind.

Due diligence may feel tedious, but it's your insurance policy. This is where you separate dream deals from hidden disasters. When you approach it like an investor—not an emotional buyer—you'll walk into your first acquisition with clarity, confidence, and control.

In the next chapter, we'll dive into **negotiation tactics**—how to make offers, build trust, and close deals that work in your favor without losing the seller's interest.

Chapter 7: Negotiation Secrets That Actually Work

> *"You don't get what you deserve. You get what you negotiate."*

Negotiation is where you turn a good opportunity into a great deal—or where you miss out entirely. Many first-time buyers are either too aggressive and scare the seller away, or too passive and overpay. But when done right, negotiation isn't a battle—it's a **conversation** aimed at creating a win-win outcome. In this chapter, you'll learn how to structure your offer, communicate with confidence, and negotiate terms that protect your upside and minimize your risk.

Let's start with the golden rule of negotiation: **the more you know, the more power you have**. By the time you're negotiating, you should already understand the business's financials, traffic, operations, and risks. If you've done your due diligence well, you won't just be guessing—you'll be making informed offers backed by data. Sellers respect buyers who show they've done the homework. It makes you look professional, serious, and easy to work with.

Before making any offer, try to get a sense of the seller's motivations. Why are they selling? Are they burned out, moving on to another project, or in need of fast cash? Someone who's emotionally attached to the business may prioritize a trustworthy buyer. Someone who's managing multiple projects may care more about speed and simplicity. Your offer should speak directly to what the seller values most—whether that's price, terms, timeline, or continuity.

When it comes to the actual offer, remember that price is **only one part** of the equation. You can negotiate based on multiple levers: upfront payment, financing structure, earn-outs, support period, handoff timeline, and even consulting agreements. Let's say a seller wants $25,000. Instead of going straight to $20,000 all-cash, you might offer $15,000 upfront and the remaining $10,000 paid out over six months, contingent on the business maintaining certain performance levels. This reduces your upfront risk while still honoring the seller's asking price in the long run.

In fact, many experienced buyers aim for what's called a **"low-cash, high-confidence"** offer. That means minimizing your upfront out-of-pocket investment while giving the seller confidence they'll still get paid in full. Here's an example:

> "I'd like to offer $10,000 upfront, with an additional $15,000 paid in five equal monthly

> payments of $3,000, contingent on the business maintaining at least $1,500/month in profit. I'm committed to growing the business and maintaining its reputation. We can close within 7 days, and I'd love 30 days of your support during the transition."

This type of offer addresses three key seller concerns: getting paid, protecting their legacy, and ensuring a smooth exit. Plus, it shows that you're not just throwing out numbers—you're offering a thoughtful, structured solution.

Now let's talk **communication**. Most negotiations start via email or messaging platforms, and often move to a phone or video call. Keep your tone professional, respectful, and confident. Avoid sounding overly casual or transactional. Remember, the seller has put time and energy into building this business. Treat it—and them—with respect.

Here are a few proven phrases to help you navigate the conversation:

- "Based on my review of the financials, I'd be comfortable offering..."
- "Would you consider a payment structure that works for both of us?"

- "If we're close on numbers, I'm willing to move quickly to close."
- "I'm really aligned with what you've built and want to preserve its integrity."
- "Let's find a structure that protects both our interests."

These phrases keep the conversation collaborative, not adversarial. You're showing that you want to make the deal happen, but also want it to make sense for both parties.

Another tactic that works well is **anchoring**. Anchoring means setting the initial offer at a point that pulls the negotiation in your direction. For example, if a seller is asking $40,000, your anchor might be a well-explained offer of $30,000, backed by clear data—like inconsistent revenue, rising expenses, or time required to maintain the business. That becomes the new center point of the negotiation. Even if the seller counters at $35,000, you've effectively pulled the price lower without being disrespectful.

Be aware, though, of **lowballing**. If your offer is too low without justification, you risk offending the seller and shutting down the conversation entirely. Always justify your offer with data. Saying, "I think $20,000 is more fair" means nothing. Saying, "Given the traffic concentration and drop in revenue over the past 6 months, I believe $20,000 reflects the current performance more accurately" carries weight.

If you reach a point where the seller is stuck on price, look for **non-monetary concessions**. Can you negotiate for extended seller support? A longer earn-out period? Access to their network or team post-sale? One-on-one consulting for 90 days? These extras can make your transition smoother and add hidden value that offsets a higher purchase price.

Another overlooked strategy is using **timelines to your advantage**. If a seller is motivated to exit quickly, offering a fast and clean close can earn you discounts. For example, "If we can close by next Friday, I'm prepared to do $22,000 all cash." This creates urgency and positions you as a serious buyer, not a tire-kicker.

Now, let's address a common fear: **What if I'm not good at negotiating?** The truth is, you don't have to be slick or manipulative. The best negotiators are calm, confident, and clear. They ask good questions, listen well, and stay focused on the numbers and the outcome—not their ego. If you're nervous, write down your key points in advance. Practice out loud. And remember: the seller is just a person, and they want a fair deal too.

Once you and the seller agree on terms, it's time to **formalize**

the agreement. You'll typically start with a Letter of Intent (LOI), which outlines the basic deal terms and shows both parties are serious. The LOI isn't legally binding, but it sets expectations and allows you to move into final due diligence. After that, you'll use an Asset Purchase Agreement (APA) to close the deal officially. This document includes payment terms, transfer of assets, seller support obligations, and a non-compete clause to protect your investment.

If you're unsure about legal language, hire a freelance contract lawyer to review the documents for a few hundred dollars. It's a small investment compared to the cost of a mistake. You can also use templates from Flippa, Acquire, or Empire Flippers and modify them for your situation.

Here's a quick recap of **negotiation best practices**:

1. **Do your homework**—know your numbers before you negotiate.
2. **Understand the seller's motivations**—craft your offer to meet their goals.
3. **Use structure, not just price**—split payments, earn-outs, or consulting deals.
4. **Keep communication respectful and professional**.

5. **Anchor with data**—don't throw out random offers.

6. **Be creative**—offer value beyond cash.

7. **Use urgency and simplicity to your advantage**.

8. **Put everything in writing once terms are agreed**.

Negotiation isn't about winning—it's about building trust and getting a deal that works. When you approach it like a true entrepreneur, you'll not only get better prices—you'll build stronger relationships and transition into ownership with the seller's full support.

In the next chapter, we'll cover what to do in the **first 30 days after you buy a business**—how to avoid common mistakes, maintain momentum, and set yourself up for long-term success.

Chapter 8: What to Do the First 30 Days After You Buy

"You don't have to rebuild the business—you just have to learn it, protect it, and prepare it to grow."

You closed the deal. Congratulations—you're now the proud owner of an online business. But the work is far from over. In fact, the first 30 days are arguably the most critical period of your ownership. These early days set the tone for everything that comes next. A sloppy handoff can lead to missed revenue, unhappy customers, and burned-out motivation. A well-managed transition, on the other hand, can protect your investment, preserve momentum, and position you for fast, focused growth.

This chapter is your 30-day onboarding roadmap. We'll walk through the exact steps you should take the moment you take over—from stabilizing the business, to learning the systems, to preparing for optimization. The goal is not to change everything right away. The goal is to **understand the machine before you try to modify it**.

Week 1: Stabilize and Take Control

The first step is access. Make sure all digital assets have been successfully transferred. This includes domain names, hosting, website backend (like WordPress or Shopify), email accounts, ad accounts, customer relationship management tools, social media logins, product files, payment gateways (Stripe, PayPal, Gumroad), and any third-party integrations. Create a master login sheet and use a password manager to stay organized.

Once you have access, the next step is confirmation. Check that all systems are running as expected. Are the checkout pages working? Are emails still being delivered? Are affiliate links active? Are scheduled automations firing correctly? Run a test purchase to ensure the full buyer journey works from start to finish. This is your **baseline audit**. If anything is broken, fix it immediately—or reach out to the seller if part of your agreement includes transition support.

During this week, it's also important to introduce yourself to key contacts—whether that's suppliers, contractors, team members, or affiliates. Send a short, professional message explaining who you are, your enthusiasm for the business, and your commitment to maintaining its quality and consistency. Building early trust helps keep relationships strong and the business stable during the transition.

Week 2: Learn the Business Inside and Out

Your second week should be focused on **immersion**. Resist the urge to start changing things. Instead, spend time understanding exactly how the business operates. Follow all SOPs. Watch any training videos the seller provided. If you negotiated 30 days of support, now's the time to schedule Zoom calls, get walkthroughs, and ask questions.

Start documenting everything. Even if the seller already gave you SOPs, create your own version based on how you process information. Break each core task—customer support, publishing content, fulfilling orders, sending emails—into step-by-step instructions. This will make it much easier to delegate or automate later. You're not just learning the business. You're **building the manual** to run it without you.

Also, monitor key metrics daily. Track revenue, traffic, refunds, support tickets, and user engagement. Don't just look at the numbers—ask "why" behind any spikes or drops. This gives you a feel for normal performance vs. anomalies. You're training your instinct to know when something's off.

If the business includes a customer base or audience—such as an email list, followers, or students—begin warming them up to your voice. Send a simple introduction message that affirms continuity and value. Reassure them that nothing is being taken away. Avoid pushing sales. Just build trust and set expectations.

Week 3: Identify Quick Wins and Low-Hanging Fruit

Once you've stabilized and absorbed the business operations, you can begin looking for **quick wins**. These are small, low-risk changes that can produce meaningful improvements. The key is to focus on **optimization**, not reinvention.

Some examples of quick wins include:

- Improving the checkout flow to reduce friction
- Rewriting email subject lines to boost open rates
- Updating outdated content or affiliate links
- Adding an upsell or cross-sell to an existing product
- Running a limited-time promotion to your email list
- Fixing SEO issues like broken links or missing metadata
- Speeding up the website to improve user experience

These are all actions that can make the business more profitable without overhauling its core structure. Focus on tasks that can be completed in a few hours and start testing them one at a time. Measure results, document the process, and move on to the next.

This is also the week where you should review and evaluate the

team—if there is one. Are the current contractors productive? Are they responsive and delivering consistent quality? If not, start researching backup options, but don't fire anyone too soon. Stability is still the priority.

Week 4: Start Thinking Like a CEO

Now that you've stabilized, observed, and optimized a few pieces of the puzzle, it's time to begin transitioning into the CEO mindset. That means asking higher-level questions:

- What are the top 3 growth levers in this business?
- What's not being done that should be?
- What bottlenecks are holding it back?
- Where is the business overly dependent on you?
- What processes can be delegated or automated next?

Your role should gradually shift from doing *everything* to managing the vision, setting goals, and allocating resources. Even if you're a solo operator today, build with scalability in mind. Document tasks, set up standard workflows, and create systems that don't rely on you to function day-to-day.

This is also a good time to revisit your original goals. Why did you buy this business? Was it for passive income, freedom, the challenge, or long-term equity? Now that you've had a few weeks of experience, how does the reality compare to your expectations? Use this self-assessment to decide what your next 90 days should look like.

Common Mistakes to Avoid in the First 30 Days

Many new owners make the mistake of rushing into major changes before they fully understand the business. They change branding, pricing, email sequences, or even entire monetization strategies. Unless something is clearly broken, avoid drastic changes early on. Preserve what's working before you try to evolve it.

Another common pitfall is neglecting communication with existing customers. If the business relies on client relationships or repeat buyers, they need to hear from you. Silence creates uncertainty, and uncertainty kills trust. Even a simple monthly update or "we're still here and improving" message can go a long way.

Also avoid underestimating the time commitment. Even semi-passive businesses require effort during the transition. Block out time in your calendar to focus on onboarding. Don't try to squeeze everything in between other priorities—it will only create stress and missed details.

Lastly, don't ignore **mindset**. Imposter syndrome can creep in. You might feel overwhelmed, or worried you made a mistake. That's normal. Every business owner goes through it. The difference is that successful entrepreneurs keep moving forward, learn from mistakes, and surround themselves with the right resources.

Your 30-Day Summary

To wrap up, here's your 30-day plan in one simple list:

Week 1: Access & Audit

- Secure all logins and digital assets
- Test everything for functionality
- Introduce yourself to stakeholders

Week 2: Learn & Document

- Shadow the business processes
- Ask questions, record walkthroughs
- Monitor daily KPIs and trends

Week 3: Optimize & Improve

- Identify low-risk opportunities

- Execute 2–3 small improvements
- Review contractor/team performance

Week 4: Plan & Lead

- Set 90-day business goals
- Start building systems and delegation
- Prepare to move from operator to owner

The first 30 days are not about flipping the switch from "buyer" to "builder." They're about laying the foundation for sustainable, scalable ownership. Stay curious. Stay focused. And remember—this is just the beginning.

In the next chapter, we'll shift gears and look at how to **scale the business** beyond where you bought it—unlocking new revenue, creating recurring income, and building long-term value.

Chapter 9: Scaling and Exit Planning

"Buying a business is the start. Scaling it turns it into an asset. Selling it—if you choose—is how you unlock the wealth."

Now that you've survived the first 30 days and stabilized the business, it's time to shift into **growth mode**. This is the part that excites most entrepreneurs—the opportunity to take something that's already working and make it better, stronger, and more profitable. But growth without strategy can actually hurt a business. Scaling too fast, too randomly, or without the right systems in place can lead to burnout, lost revenue, and wasted resources.

In this chapter, we'll explore **how to scale smart**—by improving what's already working, expanding into new channels, and building the foundation for long-term success. Then we'll finish with a look at the **exit strategy**—because even if you're not planning to sell, knowing how to *build a sellable business* will keep your decisions sharp and your business valuable.

Let's begin with the simplest and most effective way to grow: **optimize what already exists**. Often, there are areas in the business that are underperforming simply because no one has paid close attention to them. For example, if it's an eCommerce business, are the product pages fully optimized for conversions? Do abandoned cart emails exist—and do they work? If it's a content site, which blog posts are ranking but not monetized? Which affiliate links could be upgraded or tested with better offers?

Think in terms of **levers**. A small improvement in email open rates, conversion rates, or average order value can lead to major revenue increases—without spending more on traffic or content. Run split tests. Track metrics. Prioritize actions that can move the needle with minimal cost. These small wins compound over time.

Once your foundation is running efficiently, the next stage is **expansion**. This means adding new products, services, traffic channels, or monetization models. Let's say you bought a blog that earns $1,000/month from display ads. Could you add affiliate links for high-ticket products? Could you create a downloadable guide and sell it for $9? Could you launch a mini course or email challenge? These additions can multiply your revenue streams without significantly increasing your workload.

For eCommerce or SaaS businesses, expansion might mean launching complementary products, offering bundles or subscriptions, or introducing upsells at checkout. Always ask:

What else would my existing customers buy? The easiest sale is to someone who already trusts you.

Another powerful growth strategy is **traffic diversification**. If the business relies heavily on one source—say Google SEO or Facebook Ads—you'll want to explore other options to reduce risk and increase reach. Could you repurpose blog content into short-form video for Instagram Reels or TikTok? Could you turn your email newsletter into a podcast or YouTube channel? The more touchpoints you have with your audience, the stronger your brand becomes.

As you scale, systems become everything. If you're still personally doing every task—posting content, replying to emails, fulfilling orders—you'll hit a ceiling fast. This is where **delegation** comes in. Start outsourcing the tasks that are repetitive, low skill, or drain your energy. Hire a virtual assistant to manage customer service. Use AI tools to help with content writing or analytics. Automate email sequences, reporting, and scheduling wherever possible.

Your goal as an owner is not to be the bottleneck—it's to be the **strategist**. The person who directs growth, reviews performance, and empowers others to operate. This doesn't mean you disappear. It means you rise above the day-to-day so the business can scale without burning you out.

As the business grows and becomes more valuable, you'll naturally face the question: *Should I sell it?* Not everyone wants to. But knowing how to prepare for a sale gives you the option—and options are powerful. Even if you plan to keep the business for years, building it with a potential **exit strategy** in mind will make it stronger, more organized, and more profitable.

So let's talk about **exit planning**.

A business becomes sellable when it meets three main criteria: **profitability, predictability, and transferability**. That means it earns steady, verifiable income; it has systems and processes that a new owner can learn; and it doesn't rely heavily on you personally to survive.

Start documenting everything—from SOPs to traffic reports, to customer support templates, to ad performance. Create a clean, easy-to-understand P&L statement. Keep your business and personal finances separate. And maintain clear ownership of all digital assets—domains, content, email lists, payment platforms, and so on.

Buyers will evaluate your business based on a **multiple of your monthly net profit**. Typically, online businesses sell for anywhere from 24x to 48x monthly profit, depending on the niche, age, growth, and risk. So, a business earning

$3,000/month could sell for $75,000 to $125,000—or more. This is where your hard work in optimization and system-building pays off. If your business can run without you and still make money, it's worth a lot more.

There are several places to list your business when you're ready to sell: Flippa for smaller deals, Empire Flippers and Quiet Light for six-figure exits, and MicroAcquire (now Acquire.com) for software and recurring-revenue companies. These platforms usually provide tools and brokers to help with valuation, listing, and the sales process.

But here's something powerful to consider: you don't have to sell 100% of your business. Many buyers are open to **partial acquisitions**, where they buy 60–80% of the business, keep you on as an advisor, and pay you a lump sum plus ongoing profit share. This can be the best of both worlds—you get capital, de-risk your investment, and still benefit from future upside.

Another option is to keep the business and use it as **collateral**. Lenders are becoming more open to financing based on digital asset value. You could use a profitable online business to secure a business line of credit, invest in other acquisitions, or fund the launch of a new brand.

Let's recap how to think about scaling and exit:

1. **Optimize before expanding** – Small tweaks to conversion or retention can double your profit.

2. **Expand with strategy** – Add products, traffic sources, and monetization channels that align with the audience.

3. **Build systems and delegate** – Document everything and stop being the only operator.

4. **Plan your exit in advance** – Even if you don't sell now, build the business as if you might.

5. **Know your options** – Sell all, sell part, or leverage your asset for more capital.

Remember, owning a business isn't just about monthly income. It's about **building equity**. You now control an appreciating digital asset that can be sold, partnered, licensed, or scaled in dozens of directions.

This is the true power of acquiring online businesses. You didn't start from scratch. You skipped the guesswork. You bought something that already worked—and made it better. That's not just leverage. That's legacy.

In the final chapter, we'll wrap up with a bonus section: Creative Ways to Fund Your First (or Next) Acquisition, where you'll learn funding strategies that help you grow even faster, with minimal capital and smarter risk.

Chapter 10: Creative Ways to Fund Your First (or Next) Acquisition

> *"Lack of money isn't the problem. Lack of strategy is."*

One of the most common reasons people don't take action on buying their first online business is simple: **they think they can't afford it.** It's easy to look at a $15,000 or $30,000 listing and immediately rule yourself out. But the truth is, there are **dozens of creative ways to fund an acquisition**, even if you don't have a big savings account or access to traditional business loans.

In this chapter, we're going to break the "I need money to make money" myth and explore real-world strategies that beginner and intermediate buyers use every day to acquire online businesses with **little to no upfront capital**. Some of these approaches involve alternative financing. Others rely on negotiation. And a few use assets you already have—even if you don't realize it yet.

Let's begin with the most common approach: **seller financing**. We discussed this briefly in Chapter 5, but now let's dig deeper. Seller financing is when the seller agrees to receive part of the payment upfront and the rest over time. In the online business world, this is more common than you think—especially with motivated sellers. For example, if a business is listed for $20,000, you might offer $8,000 upfront and pay the remaining $12,000 in $1,000 monthly payments over a year. The business income can cover those payments if it's cash flowing from day one. This structure allows you to **leverage the asset to fund itself.**

Many sellers will consider this if you present yourself professionally, prove you've done your homework, and offer reasonable terms. They're not just selling the business—they're buying your ability to take care of it. If the business has recurring revenue and strong fundamentals, they're more likely to feel secure in a seller-financed deal.

Another strategy is using a **performance-based earn-out**. In this model, you agree to pay the seller a portion of future profits based on the business meeting certain milestones. For example, you pay $5,000 upfront and agree to pay 30% of net profits until the seller receives the full asking price. This lowers your risk while allowing the seller to participate in future upside. Earn-outs work best when the business has fluctuating revenue or unproven recent growth—because you're sharing the risk.

Next, let's talk about **business credit and lines of credit**.

If you already own an LLC, even if it's brand new, you can start building business credit. Apply for vendor accounts (Net-30 terms), establish a relationship with a business-friendly bank or credit union, and consider a 0% APR business credit card. Many of these offer 6–12 months of no interest, which can be used to purchase a business and pay it off with incoming revenue before interest ever hits.

Alternatively, if you have strong **personal credit**, you can use a 0% introductory APR credit card to finance the deal. Some cards allow balance transfers or give you access to a checking account where you can deposit funds directly. This is not without risk, but if you're buying a business with consistent, reliable cash flow, it can be a low-cost way to finance your first acquisition.

Another powerful—and often overlooked—option is to **partner with someone**. If you don't have the funds but have the time and skills, find an investor who does. You bring the operational knowledge, due diligence process, and time commitment. They bring the capital. You split ownership or profits based on agreed terms. Many investors want passive income from online businesses but don't have the bandwidth to run them. You can become the operator they're looking for.

Start with your own network—family, friends, local business

owners. You'd be surprised how many people are sitting on capital and open to investing in a simple, cash-flowing business if they trust the operator. Offer them 50% of profits, or equity with a preferred return on investment, or a fixed buyout after 24 months. Structure the deal however it makes sense—just make sure it's in writing and includes clear expectations.

Let's also explore **acquisition entrepreneurship through retirement funds**. If you have a 401(k) or IRA from a previous employer, you can roll it over into a **self-directed IRA** or **ROBS (Rollover as Business Startup)** plan. This allows you to use retirement funds to invest in or buy a business—without penalties or taxes. You'll need to work with a custodian or ROBS specialist, but it's a powerful strategy for tapping into capital you already have.

Another funding route is through **government or SBA loans**, though this can be trickier with online businesses. The Small Business Administration is more accustomed to traditional brick-and-mortar deals. However, if the business has tax returns, strong financials, and a U.S.-based entity, it may qualify for an SBA 7(a) loan. Keep in mind, this process is more time-consuming and paperwork-heavy, but the loans can go up to $5 million with favorable terms.

You can also look into **platform financing** options. Some business marketplaces like **Flippa Finance** or **Acquire.com partners** offer loan or financing solutions directly through their platform or a third party. These are often structured like equipment financing—secured by the business assets or future cash flow. You'll typically need to show income from another source or previous business experience, but it's another door worth knocking on.

Now let's get really creative. If you already own an income-generating digital asset—like a blog, a course, a YouTube channel, or a cash-flowing Etsy shop—you can **leverage that asset as a financial tool.** For example, if you have a course business making $2,000/month, you can pitch it to an investor or partner and say: "I'm using this cash flow to acquire a second business, and I'm offering 25% equity in both in exchange for $15,000 in capital."

Or, if your existing business has a Stripe or PayPal account, you can qualify for **revenue-based financing**—which is a form of loan repaid as a percentage of daily or weekly sales, rather than a fixed payment. Tools like Clearco, Wayflyer, or even PayPal Working Capital offer these services to qualified businesses.

Still stuck? Consider **buying a smaller business** with the intention to flip or grow it quickly. A content site earning $200/month might only cost $5,000–$6,000. With simple improvements, you could double the profit and either hold it or sell it within six months for 2–3x your purchase price. This "starter flip" strategy allows you to build capital without needing much to begin with.

Finally, remember this: You don't always need to **own 100% of something to benefit from it**. Consider joint ventures, partial buy-ins, advisory shares, and growth partnerships. The goal is to get in the game. Build your track record. Show you can manage and grow digital assets. Once you do that, doors open. Deals find you. Capital finds you.

Here's a quick recap of creative funding methods covered in this chapter:

- Seller Financing (split payments over time)
- Earn-Out Agreements (pay based on future performance)
- Business or 0% APR Personal Credit Cards
- Business Line of Credit (secured or unsecured)
- Partner with Investors (you operate, they fund)

- Self-Directed IRA or ROBS
- SBA or Government-Backed Loans
- Revenue-Based Financing (Stripe, PayPal, Clearco)
- Flip Small Businesses for Cash
- Leverage Existing Cash-Flowing Assets
- Partial Equity Deals or Joint Ventures

There's no one-size-fits-all strategy. The best path depends on your financial position, risk tolerance, and negotiation skills. But the bottom line is this: **lack of money should never stop you from becoming an owner**. Resourcefulness is more valuable than resources.

You've made it through the blueprint—from mindset to acquisition, from optimization to exit planning, and now funding. The knowledge you have now puts you in the top 1% of people seriously looking to acquire and scale online businesses.

You don't need permission. You don't need perfection. You need a plan—and the will to act on it.

Epilogue: Your Next Move

"You don't need more time. You need a decision."

You've now walked through every major step of the online business buying journey—from understanding business models, to finding and evaluating deals, to negotiating, financing, and ultimately growing your new acquisition. Whether you're listening from your home office, your commute, or somewhere in between dreams and action, let's pause here for a moment—not to stop, but to reflect.

You've consumed a lot. More than most people will ever take the time to study. You now understand things that even many existing business owners never learn. That's not just knowledge—it's power. But as you likely know by now, power is meaningless without execution.

Owning an online business is not just about the income. It's about what that income gives you—**time, freedom, mobility, leverage, and control.** The power to stop trading hours for dollars. The freedom to say no to projects, people, or situations that don't align with your values. The ability to create a life that fits your vision, not someone else's expectations.

But here's what you need to understand next: **your success won't come from more information.** The world doesn't need another researcher. It needs someone who moves. Someone who takes imperfect action. Someone who doesn't wait until all the lights turn green before pulling out of the driveway.

Yes, your first deal might not be perfect. You might feel nervous. You might second-guess yourself. That's normal. But if you follow the process laid out in this book—if you run the numbers, ask the right questions, structure smart deals, and protect yourself through due diligence—then you'll be doing better than 95% of people in the market. You'll be entering with your eyes wide open. And that's what separates those who thrive from those who merely try.

You don't need to buy a $50,000 business to get started. In fact, some of the most powerful growth journeys begin with a $2,000 content site or a tiny Shopify store. Your goal isn't to impress anyone—it's to **build momentum.** Because once you buy your first business and make your first dollar back, everything changes. You'll start thinking differently. You'll see opportunities others miss. You'll stop asking "if" and start asking "what's next?"

And what *is* next?

Maybe you buy another business and run two at once. Maybe you sell the first one and buy a bigger one. Maybe you build a team. Maybe you combine a few digital assets into a media company. Maybe you package your knowledge into a course or coaching program. Maybe you help others find their first deal and become an advisor, consultant, or investor. The pathways are endless—but they all start with a simple, powerful action: **acquire something.**

Even if you're not ready to make an offer tomorrow, here's what you can do *this week* to move forward:

- Set a clear buying budget and timeline.
- Browse three business marketplaces and compare listings.
- Analyze one business listing in full—traffic, profit, workload, risks.
- Reach out to a seller with a few intelligent questions.
- Build a sample deal structure in a spreadsheet.
- Join an acquisition-focused Facebook group, forum, or mastermind.

- Journal about your ideal business lifestyle—what you want this acquisition to lead to.

Action breeds clarity. Clarity breeds confidence. Confidence creates success.

Maybe this blueprint will be the seed of your first digital empire. Or maybe it's just the start of your journey into a new way of thinking—where ownership, leverage, and creative freedom become your new normal.

But here's something I want to leave you with: **you're not too late.**

There's a myth that all the "good businesses" have already been bought. That the market is too saturated. That it's all too competitive. It's simply not true. Every single day, new sellers list profitable businesses. Every month, people start businesses they don't want to finish. Every year, the demand for digital acquisition grows—and new platforms, tools, and funding options emerge. If anything, we're still early in this online ownership wave.

The internet rewards those who take initiative. And that's what buying a business really is—it's **claiming your stake in the digital economy.** It's moving from consumer to creator.

From outsider to owner. From busy worker to leveraged entrepreneur.

That's the opportunity in front of you right now. Not someday. Not when you feel "ready." But now—armed with the knowledge, the tools, and the framework to act.

And if you ever get stuck, overwhelmed, or discouraged, remember this: the business you're going to buy already exists. It's out there, running, earning, waiting. You're not starting from scratch. You're stepping into something that's already real. And that's your edge.

So go ahead. Re-listen to your favorite chapters. Review the checklist. Write down your next move. But most importantly, *make one.*

Because your business won't buy itself. But your future self will thank you for every step you take today.

www.ingramcontent.com/pod-product-compliance
Lightning Source LLC
LaVergne TN
LVHW022017200926
848481LV00007B/2439
* 9 7 9 8 3 4 9 6 3 7 7 0 4 *